# YOUR KNOWLEDGE HAS VALUE

AF137124

- We will publish your bachelor's and master's thesis, essays and papers

- Your own eBook and book - sold worldwide in all relevant shops

- Earn money with each sale

## Upload your text at www.GRIN.com and publish for free

**Dirk Oder, Leonard Andri**

# BMEcat, Standard of Product Catalogue Exchange

GRIN Publishing

**Bibliographic information published by the German National Library:**

The German National Library lists this publication in the National Bibliography;
detailed bibliographic data are available on the Internet at http://dnb.dnb.de .

This book is copyright material and must not be copied, reproduced, transferred,
distributed, leased, licensed or publicly performed or used in any way except as
specifically permitted in writing by the publishers, as allowed under the terms and
conditions under which it was purchased or as strictly permitted by applicable
copyright law. Any unauthorized distribution or use of this text may be a direct
infringement of the author s and publisher s rights and those responsible may be
liable in law accordingly.

**Imprint:**

Copyright © 2004 GRIN Verlag, Open Publishing GmbH
Print and binding: Books on Demand GmbH, Norderstedt Germany
ISBN: 978-3-656-90498-4

**This book at GRIN:**

http://www.grin.com/en/e-book/39587/bmecat-standard-of-product-catalogue-
exchange

**GRIN - Your knowledge has value**

Since its foundation in 1998, GRIN has specialized in publishing academic texts by students, college teachers and other academics as e-book and printed book. The website www.grin.com is an ideal platform for presenting term papers, final papers, scientific essays, dissertations and specialist books.

**Visit us on the internet:**

http://www.grin.com/

http://www.facebook.com/grincom

http://www.twitter.com/grin_com

Master of Science in Business Administration and Engineering
Information technology 2
BMEcat, standard of product catalogue exchange

Pforzheim University of Applied Science

Master of Science in Business Administration and Engineering

Semester 2
Information Technology II

r

Topic:

# BMEcat, standard of product catalogue exchange

Handed in by:
Name        Dirk Oder                                      Leonard Andri

_____                                      _____

Date:        June 24, 2004

Master of Science in Business Administration and Engineering
Information technology 2
BMEcat, standard of product catalogue exchange

# Table of content

Master of Science in Business Administration and Engineering
Information technology 2
BMEcat, standard of product catalogue exchange

## Abbreviations

| | |
|---|---|
| A2A | Application to Application |
| ASCII | American Standard Code for Information Interchange |
| B2B | Business to business |
| BME | Bundesverband Materialwirtschaft und Einkauf |
| CPFR | Collaborative Planning Forecast and Replenishment |
| DGH | Deutscher Großhändlerverband für Heizungs-, Lüftungs- und Klimabedarf |
| EAN | European Article Number |
| eBSC | e-Business Standardization Committee |
| EDI | Electronic Data Interchange |
| GDD | Global Data Dictionary |
| GmbH | Gesellschaft mit beschränkter Haftung (Limited liability company) |
| GSMP | Global Standards Management Process |
| SOX | Schema for Object orientated XML |
| UBL | Universal Business Language |
| UCC | Uniform Code Council |
| VSI | Bundesverband des Sanitärfachhandels |
| XML | Extensable Markup Language |
| XSDL | XML Schema Definition Language |

Master of Science in Business Administration and Engineering
Information technology 2
BMEcat, standard of product catalogue exchange

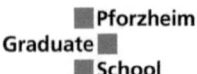

## Management Summary

In electronic catalogue interchange we have more than 160 different standards to support the catalogue exchange. BMEcat is one of the most important exchange standards in Europe. BMEcat is an open source XML based standard, developed by the BME, Fraunhofer Institute, University of Essen and Linz to support the supplier – customer business in the industry. The special in BMEcat is the wide range of supported branches. So it is possible for a company to have a look on all needed products and services to run the business, not only the production related. In 2004 we are preparing for version 2.0 with the integration of openTRANS as a document interchange standard. The paper describes the working system and the structure of the standard; comparing it to other solutions and showing up some experiences of users. Finally we sketch the future of BMEcat.

## 1.     Introduction

### 1.1     History and Background

Recently marketplace between sales and procurement has already developed into a digitalization and electronically level. This means that many companies in a different kind field of industry have developed and use their sale and procurement process to e-business, particularly big companies which have numerous number of suppliers and customers. This situation brings suppliers, manufacturers, distribution centre, sole agents, and customers from different kind of background into an e-marketplace. All of these market elements bring their products to the marketplace electronically that allow the participants of marketplace to see and study their products in more flexible way.

The environment of e-marketplace is wide-range and variously. Same kind of products is offered by different suppliers with various ways and characters to the marketplace and manufacturer/customer are searching for the most optimum supplier from this marketplace. Imagine a big company like Siemens that has 220,000 suppliers to handle offer and find the right supplier for their purchasing. Therefore, a standard of product information is needed to ease customers to have the right information about the product and also for the supplier to provide the right information about their product.

Master of Science in Business Administration and Engineering
Information technology 2
BMEcat, standard of product catalogue exchange

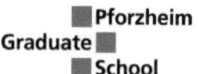
■Pforzheim
Graduate■
■School

## 1.2 The Solution

Today, about 160 electronically standards are circulating in the internet worldwide. Since November 1999 in Germany, the German Federal Association for Material Management, Purchasing and Logistics (Bundesverband Materialwirtschaft, Einkauf und Logistik eV. /BME) has issued a product catalogue standard, so called BMEcat which is an open source service. The version 1.0 was supported by leading companies like American Express, Alcatel, Bayer, BMW, Daimler Chrysler, SAP, Siemens, etc.

The specialized development partners from BMEcat were carried out by the Fraunhofer Institute IAO, Stuttgart and the universities of Essen and Linz (Austria). The official technology partners are Oracle and JAB Germany.

BMEcat offers even more possibilities for the sales side. Apart from being used to transfer data, the standardised BMEcat catalogue document can also be put to excellent use in order to compile or update a purchaser's own online shop for sales support. As the result, BMEcat will considerably reduce costs not only from the supplier side, but also from the purchasing side.

## 1.3 Development and Certification of BMEcat

Since the version 1.0 was released, it was upgraded two times to the version 1.2, and 2.0. The latest version 2.0 is planed to be released in second quarter 2004. The following figure and table gives an overview what was implemented since the first launch up to today.

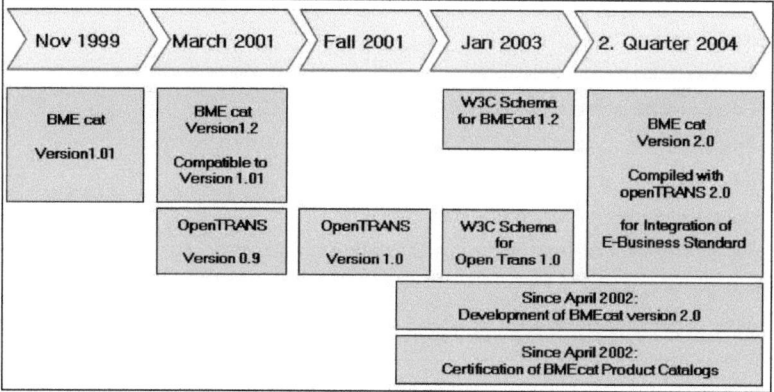

Figure 1 development of BMEcat

Master of Science in Business Administration and Engineering
Information technology 2
BMEcat, standard of product catalogue exchange

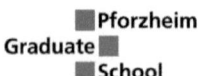

Version 1.01 (Release: November 1999)

- Extensive coverage of the requirements made of multi-media product data and catalogue structures
- Structuring of the product data in several fields, e.g. basic data, packaging data, price data, multi-media additional data, article structure data, catalogue structure data
- Recommendations for the use of standardized product classification systems (catalogue structures)
- Definition of must and can fields, data types, field lengths and additional regulations
- Definition of several catalogue transactions: for example new, complete product catalogue, updating of individual product data, updating of prices
- Possibility to transfer main data and multi-media additional data separately
- The Internet but also conventional media (CD-ROM, discs, DAT) can be used for data transfer
- Direct import into all important target systems for online catalogues used in procurement or sales
- Definition of data structures and exchange formats with the aid of XML, the standard descriptive language for structured data exchange in the Internet environment
- Simple expansion of the standard is possible to fulfil future requirements
- Users can add specific fields if required


Version 1.2 (Release: March 27 2001)

- Classification of an article according to different classification systems
- Transfer of prices for different periods of validity
- Extended possibilities for transferring classification systems
- Fundamentally revised documentation with extensions and more precise explanations


Version 2.0 (Release: open, planned 2004)

- Extension of the product model regarding complex, especially configurable products
- Extension of the product model for describing services
- Extension of the price model (e.g. multi-level discounts, dynamic price components)
- Extension of the product description regarding logistic information (e.g. dimensions, delivery process, transportation, hazardous goods)
- Support of external catalogue access (e.g. OCI, punchOut, Roundtrip)

New Improvements in Version 2.0

- Easier multi-lingual catalogues
- Multi-supplier catalogues
- Integration of the content models of BMEcat and openTRANS into one uniform vocabulary for electronic data exchange

Master of Science in Business Administration and Engineering
Information technology 2
BMEcat, standard of product catalogue exchange

If a supplier wants to take part in the world of BME cat, his catalogue has to be certificated.

Certification of BMEcat can only be obtained through the BMEcat organization by submitting their product catalogue to BMEnet GmbH or its partners such as CaContent GmbH, e-pro Solutions GmbH, Datalog Software AG, etc (more partners information can be refer to www.bmecat.org). This product catalogue will be studied and given official stamp if it's qualified. Every company who has certified product catalogue will be supported by marketing department from BMEnet GmbH by putting them into the certified company list.

## 2.      Target Groups

BMEcat catalogue standard is founded by the German ministry which targets for companies either it is manufacturer or services companies, and particularly:

1.  Companies that have numerous number of suppliers and customers companies in Germany
2.  Companies doing a lot of product catalogue exchange in Germany
3.  Companies that sells products or procuring materials electronically through the internet, e-market (e-sales & e-procurement)
4.  Companies whose materials or products are high specification and various

Looking back to the history which is driven by major companies in Germany, BMEcat at the present time is more dedicated and targeted to companies that do business transaction in Germany. But moreover it is expected also to play more roles internationally in the future.

## 3.      BMEcat and XML

The standard needs a basis that is understandable worldwide. BME choose XML as language, because content and design are strictly separated. The following chapter describes the working

## 3.1      XML as the base of BMEcat

BMEcat product catalogue is written in XML. Using XML as the basis of BMEcat, it is stated for several reasons:

1.  XML is a computer data language that can be defined or translated from any human language(meta language)
2.  XML is an open and free industrial standard, which is also well-known internationally
3.  XML doesn't depend on any special manufacturer, system or any platform
4.  XML is not  program language and has no permanent architecture

Master of Science in Business Administration and Engineering
Information technology 2
BMEcat, standard of product catalogue exchange

5. XML schema provides format that immediately, which can transfer real classification systems in all details[1]

## 3.2 The working system of BMEcat

From the BME organization the standardized catalogues can be classified into three catalogue-forms, the business transaction point of view. These standardized business catalogues are (1) new product catalogue, (2) update product catalogue and (3) update prices catalogue. As how they were named, when the very first time a product catalogue is created, it has to follow the schema from new product catalogue, and if product information is changed it can be updated through the update product schema or if it is only price information changed, then it can be updated through the update prices schema.

As it is mentioned in the previous paragraph about the standard catalogues released by BME organization, the procedure of business transaction are summarized as followed:

1. A supplier creates a new product catalogue based on XML language. Content of product and price information are refer to the standard from BME.
2. A finished product catalogue is sent to BMEnet or its official partners to get the certification.
3. After certified, this catalogue is ready to be part of business transaction; either listed in purchasing companies or directly to purchasing department of customers.
4. In case of information update:
   a. For product information update, the supplier updates the changed information in its previously certified catalogue and submits it to get the new certification.
   b. For price updates, the supplier updates the price information following the update price catalogue schema and submits it to get the new certification.
   c. The certified catalogue is ready, sending to the recipient, either purchasing company or customer

Note. In many cases, supplier companies create a product catalogue and send it to purchasing companies or BMEnet certification companies which also provide services to transform the information into XML which is already verified with BMEcat standard.

---

[1] Performed by Joerg Leukel, Volker Schmitz, Frank-Dieter Dorloff

Master of Science in Business Administration and Engineering
Information technology 2
BMEcat, standard of product catalogue exchange

## 3.3 Content and structure of BMEcat

Content of BMEcat standard is described to the following paragraph as catalogue document, which allows not only text and number, but also multimedia product data, such as photographs, graphics, technical documentation, video data, etc to be integrated.

Type of data: There are three types of data that allowed in BMEcat schema, they are: scalar data, enumerated data type and aggregate data type.

| Name | Description/ Format | Example |
|---|---|---|
| STRING | PCDATA2 | Charlie casual shirt |
| NUMBER | Numeric value. Used whenever a more specific numeric format is either not required or impractical. There are no restrictions regarding minimum or maximum values, the number of digits or the number of decimal places. The decimal separator is the dot. No separator for thousand is permitted | 15<br>3.14<br>-1,23E+15<br>Error:<br>13,2<br>1.000.000 |
| INTEGER | Whole number with an optional sign. No fractions. No floating-point numbers. No separator for thousand is permitted | 1; 58502; -13 |
| FLOAT | Floating-point number in accordance with IEEE. The decimal separator is the dot. No separator for thousand is permitted | .314159265358979E+1 |
| BOOLEAN | The values "true" or "false" can be entered, case-insensitive, i.e. regardless of whether in capitals or small letters | TRUE or true or True |
| TIMETYPE | Date in ISO 8601 format (YYYY-MM-DD) (see http://www.w3.org/TR/NOTE-datetime) | 1999-07-28 |
| DATETYPE | in ISO 8601 format (HH:MM:SS) without the time zone (see http://www.w3.org/TR/NOTE-datetime) | 6:17:55 AM |
| TIMEZONETYPE | Time zone is in ISO 8601 format (see http://www.w3.org/TR/NOTE-datetime) | +0100 |

Table 1. Standard of Scalar Data[2]

| Name | Standard | Example |
|---|---|---|
| COUNTRIES | ISO 3166-1:1997 Country codes [ISO-3166-1:1997] http://www.din.de/gremien/nas/nabd/iso3166ma/codlstp1/index.html Compare also: ISO 3166-2:1998 Country subdivision codes [ISO-3166-2:1998] http://www.din.de/gremien/nas/nabd/iso3166ma/devrel_2.html http://193.194.138.128/locode/ | DE (Germany); US (USA) DE-NW (North-Rhine Westphalia in Germany) |
| CURRENCIES | ISO 4217:1995 Currency codes [ISO-4217:1995] http://www.unece.org/cefact/rec/rec09en.htm | DEM (Deutsche Mark); USD (US-Dollar) |
| LANG | ISO 639-2:1998 Language code [ISO-639-2:1998] deu (German) | deu (German) |
| UNIT | UN/ECE Recommendation 20 (all except "Package Units") http://www.unece.org/cefact/rec/rec20en.htm | MTR (Meter, meter) |
| PUNIT | UN/ECE Recommendation 20 / Package Units http://www.unece.org/cefact/rec/rec20en.htm | C62 (piece, Stück) |

Table 2 Standard of Enumerated Data[3]

Note. The BMEcat aggregate data type standard consists of the data type DATETIME, to define a date or time. The data type is represented as an element, which itself is made up of three elements DATE, TIME and TIMEZONE. An exact description is to be found in the element reference under type DATETIME.

---

[2] See: www.bmecat.org

Master of Science in Business Administration and Engineering
Information technology 2
BMEcat, standard of product catalogue exchange

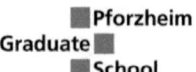

Type of structure (schema): BMEcat standard consist of new product catalogue, update product catalogue and update price catalogue. In each schema, it contains of items that are shown hierarchically. Some items are mandatory, which means they must be included in the catalogue, and some others are optional. This mandatory items are called 'must'items and those optional are 'can' items. In the schema, you may also find that some 'can' items contain of 'must' and/or 'can' items. This means that if you include a 'can' item that contains 'must' item(s), then these 'must' items must appear as the part of your 'can' item.

## 3.4    Example of BMEcat

Following is visualised an example of BMEcat content for a product of man fashion. It offers two kinds of products which are:

- man office shirt for travelling with long armed,
- man casual trouser.

```
- <BMECAT>
- <HEADER>
- <CATALOG>
  <LANGUAGE>deu</LANGUAGE>
  <CATALOG_ID>124sd34f</CATALOG_ID>
  <CATALOG_VERSION>2.1</CATALOG_VERSION>
  <CATALOG_NAME>Ein einfacher Katalog Maerz 2001</CATALOG_NAME>
  <CURRENCY>EUR</CURRENCY>
  </CATALOG>
- <BUYER>
  <BUYER_NAME>KaufWut AG</BUYER_NAME>
- <ADDRESS type="buyer">
  <NAME>KaufWut AG</NAME>
  <CONTACT>Herr Gier</CONTACT>
  <STREET>Am Markt 1</STREET>
  <ZIP>12345</ZIP>
  <CITY>Grosstadt</CITY>
  <COUNTRY>DE</COUNTRY>
  </ADDRESS>
  </BUYER>
- <SUPPLIER>
  <SUPPLIER_NAME>HatAlles GmbH</SUPPLIER_NAME>
- <ADDRESS type="supplier">
  <NAME>HatAlles GmbH</NAME>
  <STREET>Hinterm Dorf 7</STREET>
```

---

[3] See: www.bmecat.org

Master of Science in Business Administration and Engineering
Information technology 2
BMEcat, standard of product catalogue exchange

```
<ZIP>54321</ZIP>
<CITY>Kleinstadt</CITY>
<COUNTRY>DE</COUNTRY>
</ADDRESS>
</SUPPLIER>
</HEADER>
<T_NEW_CATALOG prev_version="119">
<CATALOG_GROUP_SYSTEM>
<GROUP_SYSTEM_ID>KBK-1/200</GROUP_SYSTEM_ID>
<GROUP_SYSTEM_NAME>Herrenmode</GROUP_SYSTEM_NAME>
<CATALOG_STRUCTURE type="root">
<GROUP_ID>1</GROUP_ID>
<GROUP_NAME>Herrenbekleidung</GROUP_NAME>
<PARENT_ID>0</PARENT_ID>
</CATALOG_STRUCTURE>
<CATALOG_STRUCTURE type="node">
<GROUP_ID>2</GROUP_ID>
<GROUP_NAME>Oberbekleidung</GROUP_NAME>
<PARENT_ID>1</PARENT_ID>
</CATALOG_STRUCTURE>
<CATALOG_STRUCTURE type="node">
<GROUP_ID>3</GROUP_ID>
<GROUP_NAME>Unterbekleidung</GROUP_NAME>
<PARENT_ID>1</PARENT_ID>
</CATALOG_STRUCTURE>
<CATALOG_STRUCTURE type="leaf">
<GROUP_ID>4</GROUP_ID>
<GROUP_NAME>Hemden</GROUP_NAME>
<PARENT_ID>2</PARENT_ID>
</CATALOG_STRUCTURE>
<CATALOG_STRUCTURE type="leaf">
<GROUP_ID>5</GROUP_ID>
<GROUP_NAME>Hosen</GROUP_NAME>
<PARENT_ID>2</PARENT_ID>
</CATALOG_STRUCTURE>
<CATALOG_STRUCTURE type="leaf">
<GROUP_ID>6</GROUP_ID>
<GROUP_NAME>Struempfe</GROUP_NAME>
<PARENT_ID>3</PARENT_ID>
</CATALOG_STRUCTURE>
</CATALOG_GROUP_SYSTEM>
<ARTICLE>
<SUPPLIER_AID>1245DF</SUPPLIER_AID>
<ARTICLE_DETAILS>
<DESCRIPTION_SHORT>Business-Hemd</DESCRIPTION_SHORT>
```

Master of Science in Business Administration and Engineering
Information technology 2
BMEcat, standard of product catalogue exchange

```
<DESCRIPTION_LONG>Das Business-Hemd fuer den Manager von heute. Buegelfrei und daher
gut fuer Reisen geeignet.</DESCRIPTION_LONG>
</ARTICLE_DETAILS>
- <ARTICLE_ORDER_DETAILS>
<ORDER_UNIT>PK</ORDER_UNIT>
<CONTENT_UNIT>C62</CONTENT_UNIT>
<NO_CU_PER_OU>1</NO_CU_PER_OU>
</ARTICLE_ORDER_DETAILS>
- <ARTICLE_PRICE_DETAILS>
- <ARTICLE_PRICE price_type="net_list">
<PRICE_AMOUNT>129</PRICE_AMOUNT>
<PRICE_CURRENCY>DEM</PRICE_CURRENCY>
</ARTICLE_PRICE>
- <ARTICLE_PRICE price_type="net_list">
<PRICE_AMOUNT>65.95</PRICE_AMOUNT>
<PRICE_CURRENCY>EUR</PRICE_CURRENCY>
</ARTICLE_PRICE>
</ARTICLE_PRICE_DETAILS>
- <MIME_INFO>
- <MIME>
<MIME_TYPE>image/jpeg</MIME_TYPE>
<MIME_SOURCE>business_hemd.jpg</MIME_SOURCE>
<MIME_PURPOSE>normal</MIME_PURPOSE>
</MIME>
</MIME_INFO>
</ARTICLE>
- <ARTICLE>
<SUPPLIER_AID>74653</SUPPLIER_AID>
- <ARTICLE_DETAILS>
<DESCRIPTION_SHORT>Freizeithose lang</DESCRIPTION_SHORT>
<DESCRIPTION_LONG>Die legere Baumwoll-Freizeithose fuer den
Mann.</DESCRIPTION_LONG>
</ARTICLE_DETAILS>
- <ARTICLE_ORDER_DETAILS>
<ORDER_UNIT>PK</ORDER_UNIT>
<CONTENT_UNIT>C62</CONTENT_UNIT>
<NO_CU_PER_OU>1</NO_CU_PER_OU>
</ARTICLE_ORDER_DETAILS>
- <ARTICLE_PRICE_DETAILS>
- <ARTICLE_PRICE price_type="net_list">
<PRICE_AMOUNT>99</PRICE_AMOUNT>
<PRICE_CURRENCY>DEM</PRICE_CURRENCY>
</ARTICLE_PRICE>
- <ARTICLE_PRICE price_type="net_list">
<PRICE_AMOUNT>50.61</PRICE_AMOUNT>
```

Master of Science in Business Administration and Engineering
Information technology 2
BMEcat, standard of product catalogue exchange

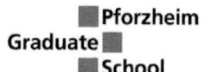

```
<PRICE_CURRENCY>EUR</PRICE_CURRENCY>
</ARTICLE_PRICE>
</ARTICLE_PRICE_DETAILS>
<MIME_INFO>
<MIME>
<MIME_TYPE>image/jpeg</MIME_TYPE>
<MIME_SOURCE>freizeit_hose.jpg</MIME_SOURCE>
<MIME_PURPOSE>normal</MIME_PURPOSE>
</MIME>
</MIME_INFO>
</ARTICLE>
<ARTICLE_TO_CATALOGGROUP_MAP>
<ART_ID>1245DF</ART_ID>
<CATALOG_GROUP_ID>4</CATALOG_GROUP_ID>
</ARTICLE_TO_CATALOGGROUP_MAP>
<ARTICLE_TO_CATALOGGROUP_MAP>
<ART_ID>112345vsdfg</ART_ID>
<CATALOG_GROUP_ID>4</CATALOG_GROUP_ID>
</ARTICLE_TO_CATALOGGROUP_MAP>
<ARTICLE_TO_CATALOGGROUP_MAP>
<ART_ID>74653</ART_ID>
<CATALOG_GROUP_ID>5</CATALOG_GROUP_ID>
</ARTICLE_TO_CATALOGGROUP_MAP>
</T_NEW_CATALOG>
</BMECAT>
```

## 3.5 Compatibility between openTRANS and BMEcat

Since January 2003, a new development was released by the BME organization, the compatibility between BMEcat and openTRANS. After an evaluation process the e-Business Standardization Committee (eBSC) has published the XML-Schema versions of its two e-business standards BMEcat 1.2 and openTRANS 1.0. They enable an extensive verification of the content of product catalogues and business documents. Now it is possible to make an automatically check of whether dates, prices or descriptions are in the right format. Hence often made errors in inter-company data exchange can be avoided. This results in an improved or even frictionless exchange of product data and transaction data between suppliers, buyers, electronic marketplaces and portals. But this advancement does not mean that BMEcat is a requirement of using openTRANS.

Master of Science in Business Administration and Engineering
Information technology 2
BMEcat, standard of product catalogue exchange

## 4.    BMEcat and other solutions

The BMEcat standard is not the only standard on the market. The being of internet B2B solutions is older then the standard. There is a natural historically background behind that. Every platform was using its own standard. Each bigger company was developing its own standard to diverse from other companies and to establish the importance of the own product. In the following chapter the most important standards are explained and how the interaction with BMEcat is working. Here we differ between XML-based standards and other programming-languages.

### 4.1    XML based standards

–    cXML[4]

The commerce – XML standard is used by buying organisations, service-providers and intermediaries. The standard is combining the catalogue format and a communication tool. Like BMEcat, the standard is open-source and free for everyone. The users are able to use cXML in three ways. A static catalogue, which is containing nearly the same components as BMEcat does. Second item is the purchase orders, which is similar to the BMEcat combination with openTRANS. Third, the interactive description and pricing tool, the punchOut module. This module allows the communication between customers and suppliers. This is the most interesting part of cXML. The catalogue data only contains the basic data like the classification, the articles and the hierarchy. The updating of the data can be done in two ways. First the creation of a new catalogue or second over the pounchOut-tool. Here the article-text and pricing is a file on the supplier's data base and the supplier is getting the information over the internet. This pounchOut function is very interesting for branches that have day by day prices.

–    xCBL[5]

This standard is developed as a combination of common business elements. It is not a single standard. It combines a few EDI semantics like EDIFACT and X12. That reduces the investment-costs of implementing the standard catalogue-document and makes it interesting for smaller companies. First the standard was related to the OASIS UBL standard library and SOX. Now on version 4.0 the standard is completely open and compliant to UBL. On the latest version the standard is using the XSDL schema as the canonical form. xCBL is supporting a wide range of standard e-business scenarios and contains nearly all common documents in e-business. It is compatible to ERP-systems and other standards like RosettaNet and OBI. The standard is written in many XML-formats to support as many applications and tools as possible.

---

[4] See: http://www.cxml.org

[5] See: http://www.xCBL.org

Master of Science in Business Administration and Engineering
Information technology 2
BMEcat, standard of product catalogue exchange

- Open Applications Group[6]

  The group is a non-profit consortium of IBM, Sun Microsystems, NEC, Oracle and many more. The OAG is the largest publisher of XML based content for business software interoperability in the world. The framework of consensus to ensure this interoperability in application software is based on XML. In future the standard will ensure a dialog not only between B2B but also the A2A communication. The vision is to make applications communication with each other over a general XML interface like a computer is communicating with its hardware over the API interface.

- EAN.UCC[7]

  The cooperation between these two organisations got an easy target: "Global, open standards benefit all users". EAN.UCC standardises bar codes, EDI transaction sets, XML schemas and other supply chain solutions. The description of all standards is summarised in the Global Data Dictionary (GDD). For the CPFR and Simple-eb applications the EAN.UCC created an own XML schema. It is supporting the business messaging between the related systems.

Finally it seems that the BMEcat is the most developed standard on XML-basis. The competitors are trying more or less to copy the standard. In some cases the customers and partners are the same branches like for BMEcat.


4.2     Datanorm

Datanorm is the catalogue exchange-standard of the skilled worker and the construction industry. It is established since 1986 and organised by the VSI and DGH communities.

Like BMEcat the Datanorm is only an exchange-standard not a catalogue, but Datanorm is based on ASCII code. The idea is to support manufacturers, wholesalers and retail in exchanging data. The standard is constructed in different data-descriptions. Beside the content, there are also descriptions about commands edited. One dataset can content up to seven different data-types, so the import with the most used database programmes MS Access or dBase is not possible without the manually encoding of the full content. The Datanorm standard is not an interface to exchange data, it is only the description for programmers to help the creation of the interface.

---

[6] See: http://www.openapplications.org
[7] See: http://www.ean-ucc.org

Master of Science in Business Administration and Engineering
Information technology 2
BMEcat, standard of product catalogue exchange

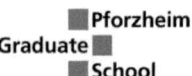

## 4.3 SAP Solution

The SAP based solution is a part of mySAP.com and integrated in the module "Supplier relationship management (SRM). Within that module, it the path "strategic purchasing and sourcing" and "catalogue management" The module is split in tree functions:

–   Organise content import: The scheme is a hierarchy of categories. The sources (suppliers) upload their catalogue in the formats BMEcat, SAP-XML or eCX to the SAP catalogue authoring tool. The catalogue authoring tool is checking automatically the content of the catalogue and will update the relevant data (e.g. prices).

–   Manage content: The catalogue manager can enrich the product data, filter and map products to an existing catalogue scheme or approve the catalogue data.

–   Create and publish the catalogue: Catalogue publishing, view defining, product searching rules.

In the SAP environment the suppliers should use all the same catalogue tool, so the total cost of ownership can be reduced. As a matter of fact, SAP supports the BMEcat scheme but the target is the global using of SAP-XML. The SAP related modules are for the SAP use more comfortable then the external schemes. Next to it, SAP customers can define their catalogue style with their suppliers and are able to force their suppliers to normalize their catalogue description. For the customer it will become easier to compare the suppliers data.


## 4.4 Microsoft BizTalk Accelerator for Suppliers

The Accelerator for suppliers (AFS) format supports the users of Microsoft related catalogues. These catalogues are using the Commerce Server 2000 Catalogue format (CS2K).

Note: The word "product" in the CS2K is similar to the "article" in BMEcat.

AFS has currently not the possibility to satisfy the BMEcat function T_UPDATE_CATALOGUE and T_UPFDATE_PRICES. Also versioning is not supported. The CS2K can build variants. So the variant "green" or "white" of a product "t-shirt" is an attribute of the product. It explains the product. In the BMEcat the variants have all the same price. In CS2K each variant (attribute) can have an own price. This is possible, because the unique variant id is build up as a combination of single attribute id's. In BMEcat each "leaf" has got it's own unique id.

There are more differences in the catalogue group systems. CS2K does not require a single root node and the hierarchy is not strict, so the categories do no have to be related to only one parent group. The third point is the product assignment to nodes. BMEcat articles are related to a bottommost "leaf". The CS2K products can be assigned to any node in the hierarchy, even when there are sub-nodes or sub-categories.

BMEcat supports multiple pricing, e.g. quantity discount or validity in time or territory. The CS2K does not support this functionality. One price is valid within one catalogue-version and one product.

Master of Science in Business Administration and Engineering
Information technology 2
BMEcat, standard of product catalogue exchange

Last content is the classification system. CS2K does not support any classification systems. BMEcat supports all multiple classification systems. It is possible to extend the AFS catalogue definition, so it can be mapped to a single BMEcat classification system.


## 5.      BMEcat experiences

More the information about BMEcat, it is necessary to find some users of BMEcat. The problem is not solved already. In many companies there are some discussions that deal with the catalogue standard. Either it is done by IT-department, because it is interfaces-orientated or it could be handled by the procurement-department, because it is a product catalogue. Some companies have built up new department, the catalogue management. The employees are specialised both in IT and procurement tasks.


### 5.1      Alcatel

Alcatel Inc. is one of the founder-companies of the BMEcat idea in 1999. The company wanted to ease the processes for the accounting-department that did all the billing that time. In February 2000 Alcatel got its first electronic catalogue based on BMEcat. The department "buy direct" is purchasing since 2001 nearly all c-parts, office material, cleaning material, packing material and tools. The experiences from Alcatel are very positive. All suppliers are able to submit their catalogues in the BMEcat standard. Sometimes Alcatel has some problems with the implementation of suppliers' information into the e-procurement – system, because the catalogue-content is not valid to the XML-parser that checks the correctness of the syntax in which the catalogue is written.

In future, Alcatel will expand the purchasing activities with BMEcat based catalogues more and more. Additionally the company will support the development of BMEcat as a worldwide standard and help the BMEcat organisation in creating key-words and synonyms to make the searching within the catalogue easier.


### 5.2      Bardusch Textile services GmbH

The company is one of the biggest service firms in textile-lending-services in Europe. Customers are many branches (Industry, Banking, Insurances, Universities, etc). Bardusch is one of the first companies using BMEcat as a standard for data exchange. In the first period the expectations of all parties (Bardusch's customers and suppliers) were very high. They were not satisfied that the acceptance of the detailed information within the standard was very low. Another problem was the requirements from the customers.

Master of Science in Business Administration and Engineering
Information technology 2
BMEcat, standard of product catalogue exchange

Most of them wanted different data-field styles and data-contents. Bardusch accepted these demands, but then they realised that they will not get to an end with this situation. After a conference with all important suppliers and customers, they decided to use BMEcat standard as how it is published. Now Bardusch works very well with the catalogue management and even the integration of SAP data and the implementation of openTRANS for the ordering is working very well.

## 5.3 Philips Lights

Philips Lights is BMEcat user since two years now (version 1.2) with the classification of eClass 4.0 (5.0). During the implementation there were a lot of problems with the company's customers, they were not able to read the data. In light bulb branch the catalogue standard range is not wide enough. Most of the customers are implementing own definitions, so the catalogue is not in a standard anymore. Another problem was the communication between the light bulb industries; it isn't clear what the competitors are doing within the catalogue standardisation. This behaviour had slow down the process. More than this, the competitors and suppliers of light bulb industry had a bunch of fears to trust in a full automatic system. That time only 10% of the suppliers were able to support the BMEcat fully. This rate became a little better with the certification.

Retrospective to the BMEcat implementation was a step to make the processes more transparent. The catalogue exchange becomes faster and the position in the market safer. Another advantage is the speed of catalogue visualisation.

Last problem now are the BMEcat-catalogue related documents. The import of a catalogue update is always given orally. If the customer is not importing the new data, there are no changes. This problem will be eliminated with the launch of version 2.0.

Master of Science in Business Administration and Engineering
Information technology 2
BMEcat, standard of product catalogue exchange

## 6.      Conclusion and future of BMEcat

Since the foundation in 1999, BMEcat has made some development, from version 1.01 to version 1.2 and even preparing for the version 2.0. These developments are supported by the users from respective companies; those are major companies doing business in Germany. Important development in BMEcat is the specialisation in detailed information and the compatibility to OpenTRANS. Moreover, the breakthrough after the standardisation of exchanging with implemented systems, e.g. SAP, ERP or APO will bring BMEcat more established in Europe and even more worldwide, as one of the important tool in e-procurement system.

In the future, there are important developments of BMEcat:

1.   Further standardisation and growing of the classification in respective branches
2.   Support in A2A communication
3.   Support multi buyer and supplier (multi function) standard catalogue
4.   Fusion of BMEcat and openTRANS as a business transaction standard

Master of Science in Business Administration and Engineering
Information technology 2
BMEcat, standard of product catalogue exchange

## Sources

BME: www.bme.de

BMEcat Organization: www.bmecat.org

Computerwoche: http://www.computerwoche.de/index.cfm?pageid=267&type=ArtikelDetail&id=80103626

EAN: http://www.ean.de/ean/Inhalt/e29/e38

Microsoft BizTalk Accelerator for suppliers: http://msdn.microsoft.com/library/en-us/dnmsse/msse_bmecat.asp

Philips Lights: Alexander Platzbecker, Mail: Alexander.platzbecker@philips.com

SAP Solution Map: http://www.sap.com/germany/solutions/scm/solutionmap.asp

Warum elektronische Standards? In: Beschaffung Aktuell: 2003, Heft 11, Page 47